EDGE BOOKS

AMERICAN SHORTHAIR CATS

by Joanne Mattern

CAPSTONE PRESS
a capstone imprint

Edge Books are published by Capstone Press,
151 Good Counsel Drive, P.O. Box 669, Mankato, Minnesota 56002.
www.capstonepub.com

Books published by Capstone Press are manufactured with paper containing at least 10 percent post-consumer waste.

Library of Congress Cataloging-in-Publication Data
Mattern, Joanne, 1963–
American shorthair cats / by Joanne Mattern.
p. cm.
Includes bibliographical references and index.
Summary: "Describes the history, physical features, temperament, and care of the American Shorthair cat breed"—Provided by publisher.
ISBN 978-1-4296-6628-2 (library binding)
1. American shorthair cat—Juvenile literature. I. Title.
SF449.A45M283 2011
636.8'22—dc22 2010035021

Editorial Credits
Connie R. Colwell and Anthony Wacholtz, editors; Heidi Thompson, designer; Wanda Winch, media researcher; Eric Manske, production specialist

Photo Credits
Getty Images: Mario Tama, 12; Photo by Fiona Green, cover, 5, 6, 9, 19, 21, 23, 25, 27, 29; Ron Kimball Stock: Ron Kimball, 11, 15, 16, 17, 18

Printed in the United States of America in Stevens Point, Wisconsin.
092010 005934WZS11

TABLE OF CONTENTS

Chapter 1
America's Feline

The American Shorthair is one of North America's oldest cat breeds. These cats have calm, affectionate personalities. They enjoy being around people and have no problem jumping into your lap for attention. They love to get exercise and play with cat toys. American Shorthairs also tend to be healthy and rarely need special care. Because of their short coats, they tend not to shed as much as some other cat breeds. These qualities make the breed one of the most popular in North America.

In 2009 the American Shorthair was the eighth most popular breed in the Cat Fanciers' Association (CFA). The CFA is the world's largest cat registry. The organization recognizes more than 40 cat breeds.

breed—a certain kind of animal within an animal group; breed also means to mate and raise a certain kind of animal

registry—an organization that keeps track of the ancestry for cats of a certain breed

An American Shorthair's wide eyes and round face give it a friendly appearance.

American Shorthairs are playful and enjoy being near people.

FACT: The American Shorthair is consistently among the top 10 most popular cat breeds according to the CFA.

IS AN AMERICAN SHORTHAIR RIGHT FOR YOU?

If you're looking for a good-natured, affectionate cat to call your own, the American Shorthair makes a great family pet. These cats are loyal companions that tend to enjoy the company of children and dogs.

People who want to own an American Shorthair can buy one from a quality breeder. Breeders make sure their cats are healthy. A breeder usually owns one or both of the kitten's parents. Many owners like to meet the kitten's parents. They can learn how the kitten might look and behave when it is grown.

You can also try to adopt an American Shorthair at your local animal shelter. The cat's medical history might not be known at an animal shelter. Still, it can be an inexpensive place to get a lovable pet who needs a home.

AMERICAN SHORTHAIR HISTORY

The American Shorthair is one of the few cat breeds that developed in North America. Shorthaired cats came to the continent with early explorers and settlers from Europe. The cats caught rats and mice on the ships.

Many historians believe the Pilgrims brought cats aboard the Mayflower. The American Shorthair breed is a descendant of these early North American cats.

A NEW BREED

People in North America used shorthaired cats to rid their houses and barns of rats and mice. In the late 1800s, they wanted cats for a different reason. People became interested in breeding and showing cats.

Siamese and longhaired cats were brought to North America from Europe and Asia. These cats were sometimes allowed to run free and mate with the native shorthaired cats. The resulting kittens often looked much different than the shorthaired cats.

descendant—an animal's offspring and family members born to those offspring

native—a person, an animal, or a plant that originally lived or grew in a certain place

The first Shorthairs were nicknamed "mousers" because of their ability to catch mice.

FACT: More than 100 years ago, an American Shorthair was priced at $2,500 at a cat show. That's equal to about $63,000 today!

Some people wanted to preserve the native shorthaired breed. They chose shorthaired cats with the best qualities, such as a tough coat, and began to breed them. They called the breed the Shorthair. Later, the breed's name was changed to the Domestic Shorthair.

GAINING RESPECT

In 1906 the CFA included the Domestic Shorthair as one of the first five recognized cat breeds. For many years, the CFA's recognition didn't help the Domestic Shorthair's popularity. The cats received little respect and attention from cat show judges and breeders. They preferred breeds from other countries, such as the Persian and the Siamese. Domestic Shorthairs could only compete in the household pets class at many cat shows. Cat clubs often did not provide cages or trophies for Domestic Shorthairs at cat shows.

Today's American Shorthairs are the result of careful breeding more than a century ago.

Some cats perform tricks and routines at cat shows.

The Domestic Shorthair breed began to gain respect during the 1960s. In 1964 a silver cat named Shawnee Sixth Son won the CFA's Kitten of the Year award. Shawnee won another award, Cat of the Year, the following year.

In 1966 breeders voted to change the breed's name from Domestic Shorthair to American Shorthair. The name was changed to reflect the breed's history in North America. Today the American Shorthair is known as a truly American cat.

FACT: Seventy-one American Shorthair cats took part in the first U.S. cat show in 1895.

Chapter 3

A CAT OF MANY COLORS

American Shorthairs are average-sized cats. Males usually weigh between 11 and 15 pounds (5 and 6.8 kilograms). Females are smaller. They usually weigh between 8 and 12 pounds (3.6 and 5.4 kg).

Most cat breeds are fully grown at one year. But American Shorthairs may not reach their full size until they are three or four years old.

BODY

The American Shorthair has a muscular, sturdy body. Its coat is made up of short, thick fur that feels hard to the touch. A Shorthair's legs and neck are muscular, but they are average in size compared to other cats. Its tail is medium to long in length. The tail starts out thick and becomes thinner at the tip. A Shorthair's broad back helps the playful breed stay active.

The American Shorthair breed is known for having large eyes, a wide head, and round cheeks. It has an average-sized nose, and its mouth is filled with strong teeth for catching prey.

prey—an animal hunted by another animal for food

FACT: American Shorthair males are usually 50 to 75 percent bigger than females.

American Shorthairs come in a variety of colors and patterns.

COLORS

American Shorthairs' coats can come in many different colors. Some have only one solid color. Others have patches and markings of two or more colors. These colors include white, blue, red, and silver. Blue is a shade of gray. Red is a shade of orange.

Many American Shorthairs have one solid color with white patches.

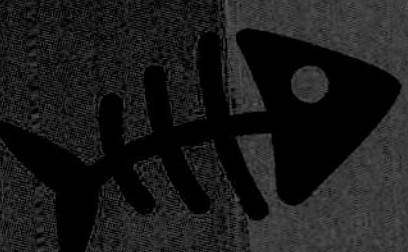

FACT: American Shorthairs' coats can be one of more than 80 combinations of colors and patterns.

Silver tabby is the most common American Shorthair color pattern. These cats have silver coats with black striped markings. They have a black marking on their foreheads that looks like the letter "M." Red tabby is another common color pattern among American Shorthairs. These cats have medium-orange fur with darker orange tabby markings.

tabby—a striped coat

Bi-color, smoke, and van patterns are also found in American Shorthairs. Bi-colors have patches of white and a solid color. Smoke cats have a white undercoat with an overcoat of another solid color. Vans have white coats with patches of a different color on their head, tail, and legs.

American Shorthairs may also be calico or tortoiseshell. Calico cats' coats have large patches of three colors. The most common colors are white and shades of black and red. Tortoiseshells' coats are a mixture of red, black, and white fur.

The coats of calico cats have a blend of three colors.

FACT: American Shorthairs are sometimes called "working cats" because of their powerful, sturdy bodies.

American Shorthairs love to play with toys.

PERSONALITY

American Shorthairs have become increasingly popular as family pets. Their playful nature and caring attitude make them welcome in many homes. They are known for getting along well with children, other cats, and even dogs. They do not seem to enjoy being alone. For this reason, many American Shorthair owners who are not at home during the day own two or more cats.

American Shorthairs are affectionate and friendly. They often follow their owners from room to room. They may sit near their owners for hours.

American Shorthairs are lively cats. They like to spend time playing with cat toys. They often enjoy chasing balls or crumpled pieces of paper. Some cat breeds are playful only as kittens. But American Shorthairs remain frisky throughout their lives.

American Shorthairs are intelligent as well. Owners often can train their American Shorthairs to fetch toys or other objects.

Although they are playful, American Shorthairs are known as a quiet breed. These cats seldom meow unless they are hungry. Their meow is soft and low.

FACT: American Shorthairs are "four-on-the-floor" cats, meaning they would rather get around on their own than be carried.

American Shorthairs open their mouths to meow, but often no sound is made.

CARING FOR AN AMERICAN SHORTHAIR

The American Shorthair is a strong, healthy breed. With good care, these cats often live 15 to 20 years. People who choose an American Shorthair should be ready for a long-term commitment to their cat.

Owners of American Shorthairs should keep their cats indoors. Cats that roam outdoors often catch serious diseases from other cats. Outdoor cats may also be injured by cars or other animals.

FEEDING

Like all cats, American Shorthairs need high-quality food to stay healthy and strong. The amount of food a cat needs depends on its size. Most cat foods sold in supermarkets or pet stores provide a balanced, healthy diet.

Some people prefer to feed their cats dry food. Dry food is usually less expensive than other types of food. Cat owners also like it because it does not spoil if it is left out in a dish.

Eating dry food helps cats keep their teeth clean.

You can also feed your cat moist, canned food. This type of food can spoil easily. It should not be left out for more than one hour.

Owners who feed their cats moist food usually feed them twice each day. With dry food, it can vary depending on the cat. Be sure to follow the guidelines on the food package.

Cats also need water to stay healthy. Owners should make sure their cats' bowls are always filled with fresh, clean water. The water should be changed at least once each day.

SCRATCHING POSTS

You should provide your American Shorthair with a scratching post. Most cats will learn to scratch the post instead of the furniture, carpet, or curtains. You can buy a scratching post at a pet store or make one from wood and carpet.

FACT: Cats use scratching posts as a form of exercise. If they are not allowed to scratch, their muscles can become weak.

Litter Boxes

You also need a litter box for your cat. Cats use litter boxes to get rid of bodily waste. You need to clean the waste out of the box each day. You should also change the litter every two to three weeks or whenever it appears lumpy. Cats may refuse to use a dirty litter box.

litter—small bits of clay or other material used to absorb the waste of cats and other animals

COAT GROOMING

American Shorthairs need little grooming compared to longhaired breeds. American Shorthairs should be brushed at least once each week with a soft bristle brush to remove loose hair. After brushing, you should use a coarse comb to smooth out the cat's fur. Be careful when you brush and comb an American Shorthair. If you do it too hard, the bristles may break off pieces of fur. They can also scrape the cat's skin.

DENTAL CARE

All cats need regular dental care to protect their teeth and gums. Without dental care, plaque can build up. Owners should brush their American Shorthairs' teeth at least once each week. They should use a soft cloth or a toothbrush made for cats. Toothpaste made for people can make cats sick, so owners should always use toothpaste made for cats. As American Shorthairs grow older, brushing may not be enough to remove the plaque from their teeth. They may need a veterinarian to clean their teeth once each year.

plaque—a coating of germs and saliva on teeth that can cause tooth decay

NAIL CARE

Like other cats, American Shorthairs should have their nails trimmed every few weeks. This practice helps reduce damage if cats scratch the carpet or furniture. Trimming also protects cats from ingrown nails. Ingrown nails can occur when a cat does not sharpen its claws often. The claws then grow into the bottom of the paw. This growth can cause painful infections.

Owners should begin trimming their American Shorthairs' nails when the cats are young. That way, the kittens will get used to having their nails trimmed from a young age. During a visit to the vet, ask how to properly trim your cat's nails.

You can buy special nail trimmers at a pet store to cut your cat's nails.

HEALTH CARE

American Shorthairs should visit a veterinarian at least once each year. Older cats are more likely to develop health problems and may need to visit a veterinarian more often. At vet visits, your cat will receive any necessary vaccinations. The veterinarian will check the cat's heart, lungs, and other organs. The vet will also check the cat's eyes, ears, mouth, and coat.

Although most American Shorthairs have few health problems, some tend to overeat. Overweight cats are at greater risk for health problems such as diabetes. This serious disease is caused when the cat's body does not produce a substance called insulin. The cat's body cannot store sugar or convert it to energy. Cats that have diabetes will die unless they receive regular shots of insulin.

Owners who do not plan to breed their American Shorthairs should have them spayed or neutered. These surgeries make it impossible for the cat to reproduce. This is important to control the pet population. Spayed and neutered cats also tend to have calmer personalities than cats who have not had the surgeries. They also are less likely to wander away from their homes. Spaying or neutering your cat even helps prevent diseases such as infections and cancer. With annual checkups to the vet and proper care at home, your American Shorthair can live a healthy, happy life.

vaccination—a shot of medicine that protects animals from a disease

insulin—a substance made in the pancreas that helps the body use sugar

American Shorthairs make great pets for loving families.

GLOSSARY

breed (BREED)—a certain kind of animal within an animal group; breed also means to mate and raise a certain kind of animal

descendant (di-SEN-duhnt)—an animal's offspring and family members born to those offspring

insulin (IN-suh-luhn)—a substance made in the pancreas that helps the body use sugar

litter (LIT-ur)—small bits of clay or other material used to absorb the waste of cats and other animals

native (NAY-tiv)—a person, an animal, or a plant that originally lived or grew in a certain place

prey (PRAY)—an animal hunted by another animal for food

plaque (PLAK)—the coating of food, saliva, and bacteria that forms on teeth and can cause tooth decay

registry (REH-juh-stree)—an organization that keeps track of the ancestry for cats of a certain breed

reproduce (ree-pruh-DOOSE)—to breed and have offspring

tabby (TAB-ee)—a striped coat

vaccination (vak-suh-NAY-shun)—a shot of medicine that protects animals from a disease

READ MORE

Furstinger, Nancy. *American Shorthair Cats.* Cats Set IV. Edina, Minn.: ABDO Publishing, 2006.

Landau, Elaine. *Your Pet Cat.* A True Book. New York: Children's Press, 2007.

Love, Ann, and Jane Drake. *Talking Tails: The Incredible Connection Between People and Their Pets.* Plattsburgh, N.Y.: Tundra Books of Northern New York, 2010.

INTERNET SITES

FactHound offers a safe, fun way to find Internet sites related to this book. All of the sites on FactHound have been researched by our staff.

Here's all you do:

Visit *www.facthound.com*

Type in this code: 9781429666282

Check out projects, games and lots more at **www.capstonekids.com**

INDEX